F

FOR KIDS

KNOWING JESUS
AS YOUR HEALER

by Rod Baker

Harrison House
Tulsa, OK

Illustrations by Stephen Gilpin

16 15 14   13 12 11 10

Real Healing for Kids:
Knowing Jesus as Your Healer
ISBN 13: 978-1-57794-708-0
ISBN 10: 1-57794-708-8
Copyright © 2005 by Roderick D. Baker
P.O. Box 701286
Tulsa, OK 74170

Published by **Harrison House, Inc.**
P.O. Box 35035
Tulsa, Oklahoma 74153

Dedication

To Amber—my winner!

Acknowledgments

Thank you to my wife, Gloria, who is the glory of my life. Also, special thanks to Pastors Billy Joe and Sharon Daugherty, to Victory Christian Center, and to the Victory Kidz Ministry staff—thank you for your support and compassion for reaching boys and girls.

Getting Started

Nobody likes to be sick. Nobody likes that terrible, queasy feeling in his or her stomach, or his or her head pounding with a fever. Everybody hates coughing, sneezing, and runny noses. And worse yet, some people have more serious sicknesses and diseases like cancer or heart problems. In fact, sickness can make life hard because it keeps people from serving God, going to school, working, and having fun.

But know this: It's not God's Plan for you to be sick!

If you know and believe in your heart that God wants you to be well, you'll know what to do when sickness comes your way—you'll know how to receive healing that already belongs to you.

Use this book to learn about healing. Read it every now and then to make sure you've got the basics down. You can even use this book to help your friends learn more about how God wants to heal them, too.

God Wants Us Healed

It doesn't matter to God whether you have a big, serious disease that threatens your life or a plain old stomachache. No matter, God wants to heal you. He never says "no" to healing. He is never too busy to answer your prayer. And His answer to healing is always *yes*.

The best way to understand how much God wants to heal you is to look at His Word, the Bible. In Psalm 107:20 God says, "He sent forth His Word and healed them." He says in Exodus 15:26, "I am the Lord, who heals you." These Scriptures are just two of many promises God has given everyone of us for healing.

In the Bible, He told the children of Israel that if they would listen and obey Him, none of them would even be sick. In fact, when they left Egypt for the Promised Land there wasn't a sick person in the whole group of 3 million people.

You can count on the fact that if God makes a promise, it's a done deal. God the Father always keeps His promises. That's why we can read His Word and believe it. If He said it, it will happen. Period.

Sickness Comes From the Devil

Have you ever wondered where sickness came from?

Some people believe that because God created everything, He also created sickness. But that's not true. He did not.

Some people believe that God uses sickness to teach His children a lesson—like a parent spanking a child. Even more, there are people who believe that God chooses not to heal some sick people right away so the sick person can get stronger in his or her faith and bring God more glory. What a silly thought!

God did not create sickness. He does not use sickness to teach us a lesson or to bring Him glory. Sickness is from the devil.

The Bible makes this all very clear in John 10:10 by telling us what the devil's job is, and what Jesus' job is. It says, "The thief (the devil) comes only to steal and kill and destroy; I (Jesus) have come that they may have life, and have it to the full." The difference is like night and day. The devil harms us; Jesus blesses us.

The devil's job is to "steal." He tries to steal your fun, your joy, and your health. If the devil can, he will try to take your life altogether. His job is to destroy the work of God on this earth. But don't be afraid; even the weakest Christian has power over the devil. The Bible says that greater is He (God) that is in you than he (the devil) that is in the world. (1 John 4:4 KJV.)

The good news is that you don't have to take sickness from the devil. James 4:7 says, "Submit yourself, then, to God. Resist the devil, and he will flee from you." When you start to feel sickness in your body, refuse to accept the sickness with the Word of God. If you do this, each time the devil tries to put sickness or disease on you, it will not stick. That way you can stay healthy.

Jesus Paid the Price

Long ago, Jesus left heaven, came to earth, and paid for your healing with His own body so you could be well every day of your life.

How did He pay the price for healing? Just before Jesus was crucified on the cross, Roman soldiers beat Jesus terribly with whips and sticks. With great force soldiers hit His back, each time tearing the skin and leaving a mark called a stripe. Each of those stripes paid for your healing.

The Bible says in Isaiah 53:5 (NKJV) that "By His stripes we are healed." If God did not want us to be healed, Jesus would never have suffered for us that way. He paid too great a price not to heal us when we ask.

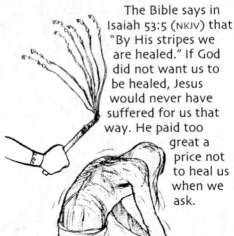

The Bible tells us that everywhere Jesus went He did three things. He preached, He taught the people, and He healed the sick. And everywhere He went, the lame walked, the deaf heard, the blind saw, and the dead were raised to life.

What worked in Bible days will work for you today because Hebrews 13:8 says, "Jesus Christ is the same yesterday, and today, and forever." If Jesus healed people in the past, He will do it today, and He will still be healing people tomorrow.

There is not one record in the Bible that Jesus ever gave someone sickness. There isn't one place where Jesus ever refused to heal someone who believed for healing.

Steps to Healing

Do you need to receive healing? First of all, you must believe that Jesus has already paid the price for your healing. It is a free gift. You do not have to plead or beg for it. It belongs to you. When faith touches God, God will touch you, and you will be healed.

If you or someone you know is sick, you can receive healing in any of the following ways.

You can say:

1. In the name of Jesus, sickness leave my body.

Every believer—kids too—has been given authority (power) over the devil. If you demand in faith that sickness leave, the devil must pack up sickness and go! (Luke 10:19.)

2. Lord, thank You for healing me, in Jesus name.

First Peter 2:24 says, "Who Himself bore our sins in His own body on the tree, that we, having died to sins, might live for righteousness—by whose stripes you were healed."

Just believe in your heart that you are healed, and healing will be yours.

3. I agree with you that you're healed in Jesus name.

Matthew 18:19 says "If two of you on earth agree about anything you ask for, it will be done for you by my Father in heaven."

Faith Pleases God

Healing is easy to receive, but there are two things you must believe.

The first thing you must believe is that God is a powerful God and He is *able* to heal you. The second thing you must believe is that God *wants* to heal you.

You cannot have any doubt about it! Your act of trusting and believing God is what the Bible calls *faith.* And even though God wants you healed even more than you want to be healed, you still have to trust Him and have faith.

In fact, faith begins where the promises of God are understood. Amazingly, God's Word becomes alive in your spirit and produces a force called faith. And faith is the one thing in the whole world that causes God to act or create in your life the very thing you trust Him for.

It's important to understand that faith works in your heart—not your head. Just because you *think* something in your *head*, does not mean you *believe* it in your *heart*. You might decide in your mind that God can heal and wants to heal, but until that decision drops from your head to your heart, it's not faith.

So how do we get faith? Romans 10:17 (NKJV) says, "So then faith comes by hearing, and hearing by the Word of God." That means if we need faith for healing, we can read God's Word to get it. Even a little faith does a lot.

Speaking God's Word

After you hear God's Word and faith rises in your heart, it's important to release that faith to work for you. Speaking the Word of God gives power to your words. Those faith-filled words can change things and even receive healing for you.

Romans 10:8 says, "The word is near you; in your mouth and in your heart, that is, the word of faith we are proclaiming."

You can speak the Word of God to sickness and you will receive healing. Jesus said, "if you do not doubt in your heart, but believe what you speak," it will happen just as you say.

GOD SENT HIS WORD AND HEALED ME!

Say Scriptures about healing out loud. Speak them boldly and often. Your faith will grow stronger each time you do.

Another way we use our faith and our words is when we resist the devil. That means we refuse to accept the devil's lies about being sick. Remember, James 4:7 tells us "to resist the devil, and he will flee from you." We resist him by speaking the Word of God.

When you begin to feel sick, speak the Word instead of talking about how sick you feel. Don't talk sickness; talk the Word. Begin to say, *He (Jesus) took my sicknesses and diseases, and by His stripes I am healed.* If you resist the devil, he must flee! You've got God's Word on it.

Signs of sickness are the devil's lies. If he can get you to believe your aches and pains instead of the Bible, he can steal your health. When that happens, you become sick. Just remember—the devil is a liar and the father of all lies. Don't focus on how you feel. Instead, focus on God's Word and His promises of healing to you! (You'll find many confessions of healing in the back of this book.)

WORD OF GOD

When It Seems Like You're Not Getting Better—Don't Give Up

Sometimes you don't feel like you are healed when you first pray. Don't give up. Don't worry. Hold on to your confession of faith. Healing belongs to you, and you will receive it. Keep believing!

When healing does not come like we expect, we need to look at our life to see why. It is not God's fault; He absolutely wants to heal you.

Maybe you didn't receive healing when you first prayed because you have disobeyed God, or maybe you are just hoping instead of truly believing.

If you have disobeyed God, simply ask God to forgive you, start obeying, and then receive your healing. If the problem is your faith, go back to reading and confessing the Word of God, charge up your faith, and keep standing in faith.

No matter what, don't give up.

Good-bye Sickness

There is no doubt that God has the power to heal even the hardest of diseases. Yet, did you know that He can also help keep you from getting sick? Sure, He can. It is called divine health. You can live the rest of your life without ever getting sick again.

God's plans for a believer is to be healthy. It is the devil's job to steal that from you. If you have faith in God, He will protect you from attacks.

Reading God's Word every day will build your faith. The Bible says that God's Word is like a medicine. If you read the Bible daily, the Word acts like a medicine to keep away the attacks of sickness that normally come. You will stay healthy.

Rx
READ THE BIBLE!
-Dr. Jesus

Your lifestyle also has a lot to do with your wellness. All of the experts agree that the proper diet, combined with exercise and the right amount of sleep, will help keep people strong and healthy.

Do not put bad things in your body like tobacco, alcohol, or drugs. It is proven that these things hurt your body and make it weak so it is easier for the devil to attack you with sickness.

Practice good hygiene. Take baths and wash your hands often to prevent the spread of everyday diseases.

If you do these things you will remain free of sickness and disease. Do them all in faith, and God will partner with you in healing and in health.

Daily Confessions for Healing

Jesus said that if I can believe, all things are possible; so I believe that I am healed. (Mark 9:23.)

It is God's plan that I would be healthy in my soul and in my body; so as my faith grows I am healthy. (3 John 2.)

I believe that the same Spirit that raised Jesus from the dead lives in me and He has healed my body. (Romans 8:11.)

God has saved me from the hand of the enemy. I believe and say that I am saved from the sickness of the enemy. (Psalm 107:2.)

God sent His Word to heal me. I have received His Word, so I am healed. (Psalm 107:20.)

He is the Lord that heals me. I am healed. (Exodus 15:26.)

I pay attention to the Word of God, and it is life and health to me. (Proverbs 4:20-22.)

By the stripes of Jesus I am healed. (1 Peter 2:24.)

Jesus took on Himself my sickness, so I do not have to be sick. (Matthew 8:17.)

I will praise the Lord who healed all of my diseases. (Psalm 103:1-3.)

Prayer of Salvation

Father, I believe that Jesus died on the cross for my sins. I believe that He rose from the dead so I can live with Him forever. I ask You to forgive me of my sins. I ask You to come into my heart and be the Lord (boss) of my life. I confess with my mouth that I am born again. Thank You for saving me. Amen.

About the Author

PASTOR ROD BAKER has served for over 20 years in children's and outreach ministry. He currently serves as director of the children ministries at Victory Christian Center in Tulsa, Oklahoma. He ministers to more than 4,000 children each week through children's church, bus ministry, Sidewalk Sunday School Trucks, and Kidz Clubs, as well as a food pantry which feeds over 2,000 people a month.

Under Rod's direction, the Victory Kidz School of Ministry is training up children's and youth workers for this millennium, while his newly developed "Leaders in Training" program is producing the same from our inner city youth. Rod has successfully taken hundreds of children on mission trips, integrating the curriculum being taught in all the children's ministries.

Rod and his wife, Gloria, reside in Tulsa with their children.

To contact Rod Baker
please write to:

P.O. Box 701286
Tulsa, OK 74170

Other Books by Rod Baker

Real Life for Kids
Knowing Jesus as Your Savior

Real Power for Kids
Knowing the Holy Spirit as Your Friend

The Harrison House Vision

Proclaiming the truth and the power
Of the Gospel of Jesus Christ
With excellence;

Challenging Christians to
Live victoriously,
Grow spiritually,
Know God intimately.